How To Become
A Successful
Consultant
In Your Own Field

by Hubert Bermont

Published by
BERMONT BOOKS

twenty dollars

PREVIOUS BOOKS BY THE AUTHOR

Psychoanalysis is a Great Big Help!, Stein & Day, 1963

Have You Read a Good Book Lately?, Stein & Day, 1964

Mine Son, The Samurai, Pocket Books, 1965

The Child, Pocket Books, 1965

The Mother, Simon & Schuster, 1968

All God's Children, Stein & Day, 1968

New Approaches to Financing Parks & Recreation,
          Acropolis Books, 1970

Jonathan Livingston Fliegle, Dell, 1973

Getting Published, Fleet Press, 1973, Harper & Row, 1974

ISBN 0-930686-02-0

© 1978 by

BERMONT BOOKS
815 15th St., N.W.
Washington, D.C.   20005

Printed in the United States of America

third printing

Table of Contents

Introduction

Much has been written about the "middle-age crisis", about male and female menopausal depression,
about the thrashing around that comes at a certain
time of life when one asks one's self "What's it
all about?". Doctors of every stripe have theo-
ries, TV panelists devote endless hours discuss-
ing causes and remedies, while the other media
join the cacophony.

True, there are biological and hormonal changes occurring at that time of life, and they are
somewhat akin to adolescence. But this parallel
is overworked *ad nauseum* - - - to the point that
the individual in question is most often strip-
ped of whatever maturity he or she has gained after weathering half a lifetime. However, the
primary difference between the middle-aged person
and the adolescent is never discussed in this
context, i.e. the anxious, frightened anticipation

of the young adult in *projecting* his future *versus* the depression of the matured person in *reflecting* on his past. Whence comes this depression (setting aside any hormonal changes, which may or may not occur)? The "experts" don't deal with this.

The depression comes from looking back and discovering that in your line of work or in your profession you may not have been the cause of your own experience. Wherever you are in the table of organization, there is some one or some board taking full charge of your actions or decisions, withholding full credit or compensation for those things you have done expertly, and overcharging you for your errors. This authority makes the rules, breaks the rules, and changes the rules - - - sometimes in mid-project. This authority sets standards at will. This authority delegates responsibility, withholds responsibility, and accepts responsibility at its own convenience. But most of all, this authority offers you and your family a living or takes it away at will - - - and therein lies the ultimate power. The threat and the promise, implied or stated. The situation is endemic to the table of organization itself.

How is it possible, then, for a person to be a part of this rat race for an extended period of time without looking back and feeling anxiety

and depression, without feeling unfulfilled and
trapped? It isn't possible. To wave it away
by typing it or labelling it "middle-age crisis"
or some other euphemism is to demean the individual who wants more out of his or her life's work
and who wants a sense of self actualization.
This book is based on the fact that this fulfill-
ment will never be forthcoming from a "superior"
any more than it is ever forthcoming from a parent
or any other authority figure. To expect it is
to be trapped in your own childhood.

There are other books which deal with "the
executive drop-out", with "alternative lifestyles",
etc. This is not one of them. I address myself
to the individual who has gained a goodly amount
of expertise and experience in a given field,
who has been aware for some time of being trapped
in an uncomfortable working situation, who realizes
that changing employers will only be more of the
same because the house rules are stacked against
him by the very nature of the system, and who has
at least once thought "Maybe I ought to try consulting".

I wish I could say that I was one of those
organizational drop-outs who one day decided that
the rat race was even harmful to rats and that
my superiors and the corporation itself could all
go to hell. However, such was not the case;
heroism has never played any part in my kharma.

In truth, after having worked ten years in an executive capacity for a company (from the age of
thirty-three to the age of forty-three), after
having brought that part of the company which
was my responsibility from $1,100,000 to $2,600,000
in sales, and after having refused a promotion
within the company which would have meant relo-
cating to a city I detest, the authority called
me in one day and fired me. The exact words were:
"You are going nowhere with the company and the
company is going nowhere with you." Although
that was the most important positive event in
my entire working career (in hindsight),
I went into total shock at the time. They really
did me a favor, but they will get no credit for
it here, since they did not have my interests at
heart. Indeed, I had done such a good job at
training my assistant that they were able to re-
place me with him at less than two-thirds my
salary.

Up to this point, I, too, had been suffering the nagging depressions, the anxiety and the
general malaise. My work, for a couple of years,
simply wasn't gratifying. But I chalked it up
to some kind of middle-age thing, having read
everything on the subject. I had found myself,
in part or in whole, in every case history I studied.

How I handled this trauma in the next few

weeks and the course I embarked upon will be revealed in a subsequent chapter of this book. The
point is that it isn't necessary to wait until
"they" do anything if you have any awareness of
your own suffering. They do it *to* you; you can
do it *for* yourself.

The unknown always produces fear. The profession of consulting is fairly unknown and un-
charted. One of the reasons for this is that
it is part of the consultant's stock in trade to
wrap himself in a cloak of sagacity and mystique.
The other reason is that there is no college degree which leads to a consultancy. The purpose
of this book is to offer a basic course in becoming a consultant. To do this we shall look behind the curtain, so to speak, and strip away
the mystique.

I. Who Is A Consultant?

1. Who Is A Consultant?

I. Who Is A Consultant?

A few years ago, I spotted a familiar face at
the airport. No mistake about it, it was Ben.
A wave of nostalgia came over me. We had been
college friends thirty years back. The head was
bald and the girth was increased, but the mischiev-
ous, pixie face was the same. Lots of bear-hugs
and reminiscences of capers on campus. Ben had
been a renegade and an upstart. A brilliant boy,
he'd had the grudging respect of his fellow stud-
ents and his teachers. But he was always in some
kind of trouble. Then the conversation came
around to "So what are you up to these days?"
Ben is president of his own successful banking consulting firm. How did that happen? "I got tired
of being fired" he said in a straightforward
manner.

Ben isn't typical. There is no typical consultant. But he has certain traits which are req-

uisite for a successful career in consulting, albeit these traits alone do not guarantee success. At school, he had a quick, receptive and retentive mind. He questioned everything - - - a bane to his instructors. He would not and could not abide "chicken-shit". He ignored red-tape. Socially accepted custom was anathema to him unless he could see some private or public good in it. He dropped out or was kicked out of a number of courses; but those in which he was interested and to which he applied himself, he was straight "A". Ben never seemed to care what others thought of him - - - neither his peers nor his betters. But he did appear to be grading himself all the time according to his own standards. Most of all, he loved a good laugh. To him, the world was an amusing spectacle. He was able to maintain this attitude throughout the war, but never ignored its tragedy. Some called this courage, other called it fearlessness; I called it a spirit of adventure. Ben has been married more than once. When things weren't right for him, he either tried to fix them, or moved on. He has never stayed for very long in a bad or uncomfortable situation. He has never found himself permanently trapped.

This vignette fairly well sums it up. If you are indecisive, dour, fatalistic, deterministic, plodding or pessimistic, stick to what

you are doing and don't consider a consulting
profession for yourself. These qualities are
listed without pejoration. If everyone became
a consultant, our whole society as we know it
would fall apart. As LaoTze put it "If every
sentient being in this world was a bumble-bee,
there would be no bumble-bees."

A consultant is like a lawyer; he is also
like a psychiatrist. (These two comparisons
will be used frequently throughout the book.)
Both must, first and foremost, be good listeners.
But like common sense, that quality is not too
common. Listening is an art. Ask any lawyer
how much money his average client wastes by
thrashing around emotionally hour after hour in
his office until the facts in the case present
themselves clearly so that the lawyer may act
intelligently. Ask any psychiatrist how often
a patient comes to him with a problem which is
not the problem at all but merely a smokescreen
for the real one; almost always. Since you cannot begin to exercise your expertise until you
know what the problem is, you must have the gift
of listening intently with both ears plus Theodore
Reik's "third ear". You must be receptive.

I have often heard it said that a consultant primarily must be an objective person. Not
necessarily. He might be an opinionated lout.
Objectivity in the human animal is automatic when

he is not emotionally involved in a problem or
situation. What is required here is technique,
not objectivity as a personal trait. Child
psychiatrists can be of enormous help to other
people's children because of the techniques they
use, even though these same techniques are un-
workable on some of their own unmanageable children because of the emotional involvement. A
fine surgeon will rarely operate on a close friend
or relative. Emotional involvement cancels out
objectivity; lack of it guarantees it. Your
technique as a consultant lies primarily in your
ability to listen receptively. Only in this way
can you identify the real problem as opposed to
what the client ofttimes thinks it is, and then
get to work solving it.

     You must question everything. Only a curi-
ous person can do this and do it effectively.
The more information you have, the better you
can work. If you are not curious by nature,
don't try consulting as a profession, because
you will fail.

     Adventurousness almost to the point of her-
esy is another important quality. One of the
reasons a client is in trouble is that he has
been doing the same things with the same attitudes for too long without self-examination.
It is possible for you to be brash without being
disrespectful. The really big assignments come

often to those who are able to run the fine
line in this area. Here is a verbatim conversation I had in an initial meeting with a prospective client, the president of a growing con-
glomerate:

He: I want you to help me build an empire here.
Me: Fair enough. You want to be an emperor.
He: I didn't say that.
Me: Yes you did. I'm not judging you. You want
    to be an emperor. Let's get to work and see
    how we can accomplish this.
He: I've never had any employee talk to me this
    way before.
Me: Maybe that's one of your troubles. Besides,
    I'm not your employee. I'm a consultant, who,
    for a fee, would like to help you actualize
    your goals.

That cemented the relationship in that instance.
I earned $5100 in fees and was of considerable
help to him. Of course, you can't take this
approach, or any other, with everyone. You
have to be able to size up whom you are dealing
with. But this in itself is an adventure. It
is off-beat. It's fun. You must be able to enjoy
each encounter. I have never met a successful
humorless consultant.

You must be a person with extremely high
standards for yourself - - - and be self-mot-

ivated enough to constantly push yourself to meet those standards. In other words, an inner-directed person makes a good consultant. If you are still trying to please "the boss" (your client) you will surely fail. The client has been self-indulgent for too long and his employees have been yessing him to death. That is why he is in trouble and has called upon you. If he can coerce or brow-beat you into doing what he wants, he has no use for you in the first place, and, even though you may come away with a fee, you will lose self-respect and then self-confidence. Remember, your self-confidence is one of your main tickets to success.

There are all kinds of books and courses these days which deal with something called "assertiveness training". If you feel you need this kind of training, forget consulting. Put another way, the consulting experience implies assertiveness. Look at the situation itself. The prospective client called you; you didn't call him. He is in trouble; you are not. He has money or "face" to lose; you do not. All of this ensures your ability to come on strong. We are assuming, of course, that you are an expert in your field, because, above all, you must be right. Your strength in this situation builds the client's confidence in you. Consider the physician who displays a lack of assurance in his own diagnosis. The patient loses respect. The patient lacks

confidence in the proposed cure. The patient
does not cooperate. The patient does not re-
cuperate quickly. The doctor is considered to
have done a poor job. The doctor's reputation
suffers. The patient does not recommend others.
The doctor cannot raise his fees. A client's
initial confidence resulting from the consultant's
self-assuredness means that there is already a
75% chance that the project will be successful
due to mutual cooperation.

Never forget that, at the very least, you
are in a peer situation. If you can't shake the
old attitude that a person in a high position
(usually the one who is considering retaining
your services) is your superior, you are in trouble.

These, then, are the characteristics of a
potentially successful consultant. But what do
you have to know?

II. Expertise

II. Expertise

"Most of us, who have been involved in any industry or profession for a long time, don't
know what we know." This wisdom was given to me
by a very smart friend and client, a lady who is
president of her own small successful corporation.
It's true. Invariably, when we come to assess our
own accumulated knowledge, we come up short. Not
because we necessarily think little of ourselves.
It is just that we have no full cognizance at
that moment of the vast wealth of information
we have picked up and stored along the way. But
if we are jogged, usually in the form of questions
put to us as consultants, we seem to experience
almost total recall in areas we thought ourselves
ignorant. It's almost as though we become mnemon-
ists. This is because we are thinking professionally - - - for money; and our powers of concen-
tration are enormous in this milieu.

23

EXPERTISE

Several years ago, I received a phone call
from a magazine writer requesting an interview.
She was preparing an article concerning a segment
of my industry which I had never dealt with di-
rectly. I told her so. She pressed for the interview anyhow. Arriving with her tape recorder the
following week, she put only two questions to me.
To my amazement, I taped an hour and fifteen minutes of continuous information. I had obviously
learned a great deal over the years in the inter-
face of that part of the industry with my own.

In my second year of consulting, I was already
earning more than I had at any prior point in my
entire working life and I was enjoying my new
free life to the fullest. One day, I caught myself thinking, "What a fool I was to have sweat-
ed and toiled all those years for the honor and
glory of a thankless corporation. I should have
been doing this right from the beginning. This
is the life." But I quickly realized the nonsense
and lack of logic in this kind of thinking. Without the experience and contacts I had gained,
and without the reputation I had acquired in my
field as a result of that experience and those
contacts, I could never have become a consultant
in the first place. In mid-life, if you really
sit down to contemplate it, you come to the real-
ization that your entire working life is the sum
total of cause/effect relationships which led

you to where you are now.

How many years of experience is necessary?
That is difficult to pin down. It depends upon
many variables: the field itself, your position
in that field, how well known you are, whether
or not you have been published in book form or
trade magazine articles, your age. But certainly no less than five years and no more than fifteen. Tevya sings in *Fiddler On The Roof* "When
you're rich, they think you really know". For
our purposes, we could paraphrase by saying "When
you're older, they think you really know". Indeed,
consulting is one of the few professions wherein
older age is a help rather than a hindrance, because most people believe that wisdom only comes
with years of experience - - - even though "it
ain't necessarily so". I had a cousin who was a
student at a dental college. The entire family
urged him on to successful graduation by promis-
ing to become his patients on the very day that
he would open his first office. Came the day,
and no one showed up. When he questioned them,
they invariably answered "Maybe when you're a
little longer in the line, Sonny."

You may feel that you know enough to become
a consultant at a very early age. But, unless
you have already racked up an impressive and re-
nowned set of credentials, you are bound to be
thwarted by "What does that young whippersnapper

think he can show me?"

Next, it is incumbent upon you to make a realistic evaluation of the marketability of your expertise, experience and knowledge. Is it saleable in your industry? To whom? Is it needed? Will you be performing a legitimate function in your field? A "hype" may get you by for a year or two (if you are clever) but be assured that at the end of that time you will be pounding the pavements looking for a job again - - - with a tremendous loss of self-esteem and "face".

Sit down with a pencil and paper and inventory your skills and your experience. Go back over your previous jobs. Go all the way back to your first job, and even before that to your part-time jobs at school. Everything was a learning experience. And this will be the first time that you will be able to synergistically use all of this learning. You won't believe the kinds of information your clients will need from you. On the other hand, perhaps you will believe it further on in the book. Everything you have ever done, read, seen and studied will come into play in consulting work.

In my own case, having come out of the shock of being peremptorily fired, I went home to think about my ten years with the company. During that time - - - and because I had spent so much time

in the same place and performed the same functions
- - - many people had come to me for advice. These
were people outside of my company. They asked everything from highly technical questions to how to
start a similar but smaller business. I gave the
advice freely, because I have always liked people.
I gave it freely in the other sense, because to
charge for my advice would have constituted a
conflict of interests. Obviously, there was a
market for this kind of service. I decided to
give it a go. I really had no alternative, since
I knew that I would never take on a regular "job"
again for the rest of my life. No one would fire
me ever again.

All I had to do was surmount the supreme
hurdle. I had to get started.

III. Getting Started

III. Getting Started

At the outset, I must confess that the worst and most precarious, if not dangerous, way to get started is by getting fired from your previous position. Ben and I made it, but I'm certain that there were outside forces (like timing and luck) which had nothing to do with our talents, that played an important role in it all coming together. In my own case, I was desperate - - - financially and otherwise; I simply *had* to make it happen. As Mel Brooks, the comic who plays the two-thousand-year-old man, put it when asked the primary means of locomotion in his primitive days in the jungle with wild beasts "Fear. Fear was the main source of propulsion". First, whether your dis_missal was for good cause or not, it will be on the industrial grapevine in no time and will hurt your reputation. Second, this situation does not give you enough financial leeway and time to plan your new profession carefully.

But the main reason for quitting your job
to become a consultant while you are still in the
company's good graces is that it gives you an
excellent chance to leave with a flying start:
your current employer could well be your first
client. This almost always guarantees a successful career, financially and otherwise. It also
makes all kinds of sense for you and your employer. He has a need for you or you wouldn't be working there today. Just show him that you can per-
form the same services as competently (if not
more so) at approximately one-third to one-half
your current salary, pointing out all the while
that he needn't continue to pay any more benefits,
retirement, social security or taxes in your behalf, and you should be retained - - - unless,
of course, he is an utter fool or some arbitrary
nonsensical corporate policy forbids this, in
which case you should have quit a long time ago
anyway.

As an independent, no longer confined to
restricted working hours, working days and a
working place, no longer required to attend endless meetings, some of which have nothing to do
with your particular work and responsibilities,
and no longer restricted to dealing laterally with
other employees, you can accomplish more for the
company than you do now in less than one-third
the time - - - and that time is of your choosing.
This is not theory; it is established fact. House

counsels have established their own law practices
this way, directors of advertising have started
their own agencies this way, public relations
directors have started their own agencies this
way, accountants have set up their own offices
this way, engineers have started their own consulting firms this way - - - the list is endless.

The major accomplishment here is two-fold.
First, it gives you a financial base or "floor"
at the outset. That initial retainer will pay
for all of your start-up costs: office rent, telephone, postage, insurance, stationery, and some
"walking-around" money to get more clients. Second, and equally important, the additional clients
will come in faster knowing that they are not mere
guinea pigs in some personal experiment of yours
to start a new thing for yourself at their expense.
They will think, and rightly so, that if you were
able to resign your former position and your company still thought highly enough of you to buy
your expertise, you must be good enough for them.
In short, you're virtually home free.

If you can't pull this off and you are either
fired or just quit, you are in the same boat that
I was in on that fateful day years ago. No cash
in the bank, a severance check for $2400, an a-
partment, a son and a car to support - - - and
no prospects. It would be presumptuous of me at
this point to offer up a step-by-step primer for

every aspiring consultant on getting started.
I can only narrate my actions at that time as
accurately as possible with the fond hope that
the reader will learn some things from my success-
es and failures and apply them to his or her own
situation.

Having cleared out my things from my previous office, I went over them very carefully at
home. I quickly realized that my desk telephone
and address book was the most important item in
my possession as far as my new plan was concerned. Ten years of business contacts were clearly
recorded and up-to-date. I wasted no time. For
the next three days I telephoned everyone and
anyone to personally let them know what I was
doing and why they could no longer reach me at
my old number. Never trust your former employer,
switchboard operator or successor to tell the
world your whereabouts. Also, "Mr. _____
is no longer with us" gives the caller the eerie
feeling that he is calling the undertaker. I must
have made over a hundred phone calls with no specific purpose in mind except to let people know
that I was no longer with the firm. It was then
I learned the truth of the old adage "Throw
enough seeds on the ground and something is bound
to grow". One friend, who operated a two-person
office in a totally different field, told me that
he had just landed a big contract which required
that he be out of the city two-thirds of the time.

He was reluctant to leave his office in the charge
of his brand new secretary. In view of my excellent previous record in training executive secretaries in my former company, would I consider
training his? In return, I could use his office
as my own at only one-third the rent (it was a
very prestigious building), I could have free
unlimited use of the secretary and free use of
the telephone; I was, of course, to pay for my
own long-distance calls.

I readily accepted and gave the nearest print-
er a rush order for stationery and cards bearing
my new address, my new telephone number and my
new self-awarded title.

I then placed a news item in my trade journal
stating that I was now on my own and giving the
phone number where I could be reached. That brought
nothing but a few good wishes.

At this juncture, the worst parallel between
a consultant and a doctor comes into focus. Like
physicians, consultants generally don't advertise
their services. It isn't against the law or anything; it's just that advertising doesn't work
effectively in consulting. So I sat in my new
office with my new stationery, my new telephone
number, my new calling cards, and even new bill-
heads - - - and it dawned on me that nobody was
going to call me because nobody knew I was there.

GETTING STARTED

I studied those calling cards and realized why
they had that nomenclature. I would have to call
on people to leave them.

I made three telephone calls to former colleagues. In each case, when I was asked why I
wanted an appointment (either by the executive
himself or by his secretary), I honestly said
that I was seeking consulting work. All three
immediately put me off with some ridiculous ex-
cuse or other. I thought about that for a while.
I tried three others, but with a different approach. This time I utilized my previously hard-
won reputation. When asked the inevitable question, I came on as a peer and said that I merely
wanted to kick around a few old and new concepts
regarding our industry. All three agreed to appointments, albeit one made it three weeks hence.
I was careful not to invite them to lunch for
fear that they might feel obligated to return a
favor. I was right on target there. I learned that
what must be overcome in these calls is any feeling on the part of the recipient that you are
looking for a favor or a job. Remember, nine
chances out of ten, he knows that you have lost
your job or quit without getting another one.
He automatically assumes that all is not well
with you. If you have ever done him a favor in
your past dealings with him in your former position, that is even worse. In that first contact, he must be made to understand that things

are fine with you and that you have finally found
your place in the world - - - as indeed you have.
He will then relax.

Having set up half a dozen meetings in this
fashion, I firmly resolved not to allow the dis-
cussions to consist of idle, time-wasting chatter.
I was also careful to remind myself that these
were peer-level meetings, not interviews. I set
to meticulously doing my homework. In each instance, I plotted the recent history of the company as well as that of the executive in question.
I laid out several topics for discussion, all
leading to what I surmised to be the company's
problems at the time. This was the easiest part.
Every company has problems. I projected the mun-
dane solutions they had probably come up with
and even possibly tried. The clincher was to be
several new approaches of my own. If this sounds
mystical or crystal-ballish, it isn't. As we shall
discuss later and in greater detail, virtually
all organizations within a given field suffer
pretty much the same problems. My own previous
employer was no exception, so I had spent a good
deal of time and effort wrestling with those very
same problems; I had also listened attentively
to my friends with other companies when they com-
plained about the state of the industry.

If I haven't come right out and said this
before, I certainly meant to imply it, even though

it sounds snotty: every consultant worth his salt thinks he is just one degree smarter than anyone else. That's how you dare to look the man in the eye and describe some innovative solutions to his problems. At any rate, I made quite an impression and assumed that I was doing fine.

So what happened as a result of all that brilliant talk in those memorable, hard-earned meetings? Did I have them eating out of my hand and did I walk away with six new clients? Not on your tintype. I struck out every time. The fatal question was "For whom are you doing consulting work now? Which companies have retained you thus far?" No point in lying; they would have checked it out. My truthful answer was received like a case of leprosy. "No one yet. I'm only now getting started. You will be the first."

Even if I had foreseen this (which I hadn't in my cockeyed euphoria over my new life), there would have been no way around it. Nobody wants to be the first to do anything, except possibly to walk on the moon. Now I recalled my cousin, the new dentist. Now I recalled the number of people I knew who tried to start new publications or launch any new kind of product. All to no avail.

I would not be defeated. The situation required a lot of pondering, and ponder I did - - - for two weeks. This produced only one conclusion.

Whatever I did had to be daring, different and unorthodox. I decided to steal a page from the life of Mark Twain, a man I had come to love and admire through all of his writings.

After unsuccessfully trying to mine silver in the desert with his brother, Mark Twain arrived in San Francisco penniless. He went to the most illustrious newspaper and applied for a job as a reporter. He was told that there were no jobs available because there was no budget to pay for additional personnel. He told them that he required no compensation, that he only wanted to write for them. He was, of course, immediately accepted under those terms (there were no labor union obstacles at that time). Needless to say, his stories were published daily and read with relish by the San Franciscans. A few weeks later, Mr. Twain marched into his "employers'" offices and resigned. They were horrified and angry. They took him to task for his unethical behavior. He reminded them that he was not being paid, a fact which they had conveniently forgotten. He was immediately put on salary and given an assignment as foreign correspondent. I decided to do something similar.

The next time anyone asked me who had retained me, I would truthfully answer with the name of the finest, most prestigious and most successful name in the business. I quickly selected this firm, made an out-of-town phone call to their

Mr. A., set up an appointment, and went to see
him. I laid out an entire work-load for myself
and told him that I wanted to do this in my city
for his company free of charge. I told him honestly what my motives were. He gladly accepted.
Loaded with the materials he gave me, I didn't
even wait until I got home, but went to work on
the train; I couldn't afford the plane. It was
necessary to force myself into a state of mind
which dictated that I was indeed employed by
that worthy company to run an office for them
in my city and that I was to work for them as
though I was being paid. I worked like hell in
behalf of that firm, setting up meetings, solving problems, making projections, and filing daily
progress reports. Within exactly two weeks, Mr.
A. telephoned me, said that he would be in my
city the following week, and requested that I
be his guest at lunch. It has been over ten years,
but I vividly recall that when the food finally
came, I was so relieved, so overjoyed, so grateful and so proud that I couldn't eat a bite. Mr.
A. had told me that they were not only impressed
with my work, but were overwhelmed by my approach
which, in turn, bespoke an innovative turn of mind.
Well, Mark Twain takes the credit, but at the
time I didn't mind giving myself a small pat on
the back, too. Mr. A. then asked me what kind of
retainer I wanted. I was in no position to consider what I was worth, how much his budget would
allow, or how much his company would require of

me. I quickly added up in my head my minimal office expense at the time, my apartment rent, food
for myself and my son and car payments and blurt-
ed out "One hundred dollars a week". "Done" he
said, and we shook hands on it. No contract was
signed. (The subject of contracts will be taken
up in a subsequent chapter.) I was retained by
that company continuously for the next six and
a half years.

That was the door-opener for me. Let 'em ask
who has retained me now, I thought. They did,
and I told them. If I was good enough for Mr.
A., I was certainly good enough for them. And
they agreed. Never mind all the kudos for Mr.
Twain and myself. I owe an awful lot to Mr. A.
He made it possible. I've told him often.

IV. Growing

IV. Growing

Armed with my big credential in the form of my
first big client, I repeated the initial process
with twenty more phone calls to prior contacts.
Again the discussion of industry problems with
possible solutions. At the end of six months,
I acquired two more clients at similar retainers.
I was now earning almost as much as it had taken
me twenty years to reach in my previous career.
Only two out of twenty calls? You will find that
this is an excellent percentage. Oh, it wasn't
easy. There were innumerable meetings, broken
appointments, dead-ends, follow-up phone calls,
and even some rudeness. But it was early in the
game for me. I had not yet learned the difference
between a prospect, a suspect and a dead-beat.
I had also not yet learned that the world is full
of people in responsible executive positions who
spend endless hours in pointless conversation in
their offices just to kill time and keep themselves

from really working.

The three projects I was working on concerned themselves with three different aspects of the industry. That made the work diversified and fun. I was enjoying it immensely. All three companies paid my monthly invoices promptly.

Then I studied my calling card again. There was that word in bold letters: CONSULTANT. But I wasn't consulting at all. I was *working*, in the same areas I had worked before. There appeared to be only one big difference. This time, I had three bosses, and they could all fire me at will. What had happened to my fantasy? Why wasn't I just sitting in my office, stroking my chin, and offering up wisdom by the hour like the Oracle of Delphi? Surely I hadn't made up this fantasy on my own. The mental image of such consultants must have come from somewhere. Certainly there are consultants in my own town who charge $100 and $200 an hour, who have large secretarial staffs in expensively decorated offices, whose appointment calendars are full and who are being constantly sought after. Who are they?

The answer to that was simple, once I doped it out. They are ex-senators or others who have previously held high government positions at comparatively low salaries just waiting for the day when they could capitalize on their contacts without creating a conflict of interest. They are somewhat akin to the "five-percenters" of World War II fame, who made lots of money by introducing Businessman A to Government Agency Director B. Sometimes they are called influence peddlers. They are indeed people of influence - - - and that influence is for sale. Or it could be someone like a former director of the Internal Revenue Service, whose three-sentence advice could be worth a fortune to a large corporation seeking to legitimately find a new tax shelter. All of these people also have the word CONSULTANT emblazoned on their cards. But there the similarity stops. None of these people have any place in a book like this. Their prosperous careers are assured on the very day that the news media announce their intentions. Their struggling days are over. They have no use for the precepts set forth in this book. They only need good management of their time and an excellent accountant and tax attorney. I taste of no sour grapes. I wish them all well. I wish I didn't have to struggle to become a consultant. But I did. And so will you.

But back to my problem, if problem it was. It made no difference what I called myself, I wasn't a consultant in the true sense of the word. Nobody called upon me for advice. It's true, there was a need for me in the working area. That was gratifying because everyone has a need to be need-

ed. I was earning a very decent living because
of that need. It was time to analyze the situation based upon what I had learned thus far.

    I attempted to discover some common elements
in all thirty contacts I had made up to that point
over the previous nine months. Here the only
true talent I possess came to the fore. I am a
musician with what is known as a "tin ear". I
can "play back" almost verbatim every conversation
I have ever had no matter when it occurred. Since
I had not yet established myself as a sage, no
one, obviously, was willing to pay me for the few
hours it took me to assess their problems accurately and offer solutions. Also, whenever I offered a plan of action to attack a problem, I was
regarded as some kind of nuisance whose only goal
was to give that executive more work. In all the
cases where I didn't score I met with a certain
antagonism. Their posture was invariably "Look,
our organization has been operating fairly well
for a hundred years before you decided to become
a consultant and come in here like a doctor to
tell us that we are sick. We cannot refute most
of what you say, but we'll muddle through on our
own, thank you." But this isn't what they really
meant. I learned much later that the above was
a complete euphemism for "I'm paid not to make
waves. You are trying to make waves here. Even
if I did try some of your suggestions, it would
make me late for my five o'clock golf foursome,

and that is out of the question. This organization is satisfied to have me sit here and decide not to make decisions. Get lost."

But what about the exceptions? The ones who retained me? What did *they* have in common? Sad to say, another negative quality - - - which helped me considerably. There wasn't anything I was doing for those organizations which they couldn't have done for themselves. This with the glaring exception of Mr. A's company which was located in a different city. My work for them required an office in my town. They saved a considerable amount of money retaining me rather than opening a facility here or constantly commuting. In the other cases, I may be downbeating the hands that fed me, but in a sense I'm downbeating myself as well. Two wrongs will have to make a right in this instance. I suppose one could give them the benefit of the doubt by allowing them the perspicacity of having costed out the work in advance and come up on the plus side by not paying me company benefits and other payroll items. But the inevitable conclusion was another big lesson in cynicism about the "working" world: Nobody Wants To Do His Own Laundry! Thus was born the free lancer. Even free lancers have other free lancers doing their chores.

The term "free lance" is traced back to medieval times. A knight who was not bound into the

personal service of any king, prince or lord
set his lance up for hire. He was, in short, a
mercenary. He was free to fight for anyone, for
a price. He owed no allegiance to anyone and
could live his life as he chose. If he was expert, he did well. If he was not, he starved
or was killed in a joust. If he didn't like
the life in any particular fiefdom, he was free
to move on.

That is the way I assessed my own situation
at the time. Did I really have cause for dis-
content? No. True, any one of my bosses could
fire me (as before), but he could not threaten
me with my living, since it was highly improbable
that all three would fire me at the same time.
It is that threat that keeps most of the working
world in a state of anxiety. The only other thing
that could send me into starvation, like the knight
of old, was being inept at my work. But I was
good, and I knew it. I felt no anxiety. I was
free - - - a free lancer. The real consulting
work was to come later, but I didn't know this
at the time. I decided to stop fretting, to go
out and get still more of this interesting and
gratifying work, and to keep growing - - - and
learning.

V. The Life

V. The Life

Is the life of an independent professional or free lancer as great as it is cracked up to be? Yes. Even greater. Once a basic living is obtained in anyone's career, it is really the lifestyle or quality of life, not the money, which produces the best rewards. The subject of money will be taken up in detail in the next three chapters. Here is a general description of what my life has been like in the last ten years.

In spite of the accommodating arrangement with my friend, I left his office after four months and found one of my own. Sharing an office was too distracting for me. I discovered that office space in any city is a faddish thing. There is always one section of downtown which is very "in" and stylish. It is the area which affords the most "image". It is, naturally, the highest rent area. It has the most expensive restaurants,

shops and clubs. On the opposite end of the
scale is the slum area of town. In between is
the somewhat transient area from which most
people are moving - - - either "up" or "down".
This middle area has not yet acquired a bad
reputation, because some very notable people
and firms are still there. The buildings are
well maintained. The neighborhood restaurants
have good and moderately priced food. But, amazingly, the rents are not midway between the chic
and the downtrodden areas. To be more specific,
at that time, office space in a brand new building in the fashionable end of town cost $10 per
square foot. The slum area cost $2 per square
foot. I found an office in a very old, but very
gracious building for $3 per square foot. For
one hundred dollars a month I had a spacious,
sunny, airy room measuring twenty feet by twenty
feet. I had a real working wood-burning fireplace, free utilities and free nightly char service. This was an elevator building in the heart
of town. Because I was willing to sign a lease
for more than a year, the landlord restored the
woodwork, painted completely, and tore down a
wall which had halved the space. He even allowed
my dog to keep me company in the office.

I brought an old but serviceable typewriter
from home, as well as a desk, a sofa and two
chairs. The library table, typewriter table and
desk chair I purchased from Goodwill Industries.

I had the floor carpeted wall-to-wall, bought
a new air conditioner, and installed a small re-
frigerator. My entire cash outlay was $659. I
have and use all of the same equipment today.

I splurged in only one area. I retained the
best and most expensive answering service in the
city. I knew that I would be keeping irregular
office hours. Each and every phone call could
be of vital importance to me at that time, having made so many contacts and dropped so many
calling cards. It was imperative that each call
be answered promptly, efficiently, knowledgeably,
and accurately. I didn't care much about "image".
But I didn't install an inexpensive electronic
recording gadget, either. I hate to be on the
other end of the line with one of those beeping
things and I assumed that others would be just
as disgruntled in trying to communicate with a
machine.

A word here about answering services. They
can be as good or as bad as you make them. In
short order, the woman on your swithchboard will
know enough to answer as though she is indeed
your personal secretary. But, just as in a regular office set-up, she will react according to
how you, her boss, treat her. I have always made
it a point to personally visit the service every
six months so that the woman sees a face to go
with the voice. She identifies more readily with

my situation that way. If she errs or is neglect-
ful, I always report this to her supervisor. This
way she stays on her toes with the full realiza-
tion that I don't accept laxity on my phone, es-
pecially at the premium prices they are charging.
When she leaves that employ or is promoted, I
repeat the process with the new person assigned
to me. Of course, when your answerer goes to
the powder room, is out sick, goes to lunch or
on vacation, the situation is usually hopeless
with her temporary replacement and there is nothing
you can do about it. By and large, I have found
the telephone answering service to be of enormous
assistance at a minimal cost.

The next important thing I did was to have
the signpainter write on the door below my name
"By Appointment Only". This was of tremendous
importance to me. First, it kept away most so-
licitors. Second, it informed anyone who might
be upset by the office being closed and dark in
the middle of the day, that this was the normal
way of my doing business and that there was no
cause for concern. Third, I was now free to
come and go as I pleased without fear or worry
that I might miss an important visit or phone call.

This freedom I keep talking about was (and
is) extremely vital to me. It was the keystone
of my new existence. It marked the difference
between my old life and my new one. It is also

something that most people don't handle too well
after half a lifetime of structure and stricture.
I took to it like a duck to water, as I always
knew I would.

Not sharing the office with anyone gave me
the freedom to act any way I pleased, from nap-
ping to scratching myself in unusual places.
It also gave me the luxury of solitude when I
required it. Not having a secretary nor paying
a high rent gave me the financial freedom of
turning away a few clients who were obnoxious.
I never once felt that I was sacrificing "image"
for this freedom. No one ever asked "What kind
of a two-bit operation are you running there without a secretary?". Organizational clients always
have me come to them; the meetings are always
on their premises. Individual clients have always found my office peaceful, relaxing, charm-
ing and conducive to good discussion. But most
important, I like to work there.

Earlier in the book, I said that the average
executive could accomplish many times the work
in a fraction of the time, and do it better. The
primary reason and condition for this is an atmosphere which allows for absolutely no interruptions.
Total clarity of thought is a consultant's major
asset. No one can think clearly if constantly
interrupted. The average working person is be-
sieged all day long with unexpected visitors, un-

expected meetings, requests for immediate reports
or action, salesmen, etc. Then there are the endless obtrusive phone calls. Imagine, if you can,
shutting all of this off. Just like that! I
did. In any two-hour uninterrupted period, I
accomplish as much as I did formerly in an eight-
hour day. And so can you. We all can. When I
don't want phone calls, I simply don't pick up.
The answering service has no way of knowing whether I'm "in" or not. A secretary in the office
does know, and the caller can tell by her uneasiness when she has to lie about it.

For other reasons, at that time, I didn't
need a secretary. I can hunt and peck accurately
on a typewriter at thirty-five words per minute.
As for bookkeeping, that required about fifteen
minutes a week, once my accountant set it up.
Certainly the sending of three invoices a month,
the recording of those payments and the accurate
detailing of my expenses didn't need another person. I was still in the initial stages. Later,
I hired assistance, but that's further on in the
story.

It is important that I work in an atmosphere
which is most comfortable for me at the time.
So, if I don't feel like being in the office, I
work at home, and *vice versa*. All of my contacts are contained in a Wheeldex file; I keep
a duplicate of this file at home. I have a tele-

phone at home as well as a typewriter. Since
my primary piece of equipment is my brain, I
will, on beautiful sunny days, haul the equipment out to the park and work there. I work
on planes, on trains and in vacation resorts.
I work in airports, the doctor's waiting room,
and in reception areas of prospective clients.
I have done some of the most creative thinking
for my clients on long walks or behind the wheel
on long, boring turnpikes.

I always work at my own pace, i.e. when I
please and as I please. When I embarked on a
consulting career I was excitedly aware that my
whole life would change. I knew that this life
would be unorthodox, and I welcomed it. Like
the song says, "Been down so long, it looked like
up to me". Well, why do things by half measures?
If I was no longer a rat in the rat race, why
behave like I was still in the maze with the rest
of the rats? Why work five days a week and take
week-ends off? Why work nine to five? Why go
to the stores on Thursday nights and Saturdays
with the crowds? Why take off on holidays? Why
hit the road when everyone else does? Why get
all my sleep at night? I certainly wouldn't be
hurting anyone by answering the needs of my own
circadian rhythms. And I could accomplish much
more, for myself and for my clients. That is
what I did. My new set-up accommodated it very
well.

THE LIFE

If I can't sleep some nights because my brain won't turn off, I work then and there at home. I have a need to "get away" at least once a month for a few days. Usually this is taken care of by business trips. I have no need for complete leisure since the joy of my vocation has made it my avocation. If business doesn't take me away, I'll take off for a few days any-how - - - anywhere. I avoid the waste of rush-hours by keeping non-rush-hour schedules. I never have appointment conflicts; I don't have that many appointments.

Up to ten years ago, I was an untravelled person. I simply couldn't afford it. Since then, my work has taken me to large cities and small towns from coast to coast as well as to Europe - - - all paid for by my clients.

This whole new life seemed idyllic to me at the beginning. Although I don't take it for grant-ed now and still appreciate and enjoy every mo-ment of it, it seems quite normal to me today. It appears very abnormal to those acquaintances in my town who see me come and go and who wonder what on earth I do for a living.

VI. The Fee

VI. The Fee

What to charge the client? A big and important
question. Charge too much and you won't be working. Charge too little and the prospective client
will look elsewhere thinking that you couldn't
be very good nor your advice very worthwhile. So
what's the right price?

When I started, the question had me stump-
ed. I went for advice. I had supposed that the
nearest thing to a consultant was a lawyer. So
I visited a friend who was a senior partner in
one of the most esteemed law firms in the city.
More important, he was a man I respected. I asked him what he charged when he first started out.
He told me that this was the only subject not
covered in his law school and that he had strug-
gled with the problem for a long time. His "answer" was no help at all. He simply told me to
honestly charge whatever I thought I was worth.

THE FEE

Although I was aware that I was knowledgeable
in my field and that I had been one of the most
effective executives in my former company, I
was now starting a new profession and attempting
to do something I had never actually done before.
At this point it would not have been unusual for
anyone to feel somewhat worthless. I'd had experience in my field, but not as a consultant.
There was no way around it, however. At some
point, hopefully soon, some prospective client
would ask "How much?" and I had to be prepared
with an answer.

A story I had heard came to mind. Possibly
it was apocryphal, but it surely was germane. It
seems that a power plant broke down. Electrical
service for a large geographical area was instant-
ly cut, causing disaster. All sorts of engineer-
ing experts were called in, but to no avail.
Finally, the top brass enlisted the services of
a local old-timer who had worked at the plant
many years back. He arrived with a hammer, went
immediately to a particular spot in the enormous
labrynth of machinery, and tapped lightly on a
pipe. The system started up again forthwith,
and power was restored. Soon after, the man sub-
mitted his bill for $1,000.02. He had broken it
down this way: $.02 for tapping the pipe; $1,000
for knowing where to tap.

As it happened, one year prior to my start-

ing my new career, I had undergone a divorce. I
went to a divorce lawyer who was acclaimed by
most to be the best in town, having practiced
divorce law exclusively for over forty years.
I presented my case to him and asked his fee.
I remember at the time I had $1100 in the bank
- - - my total assets. He floored me with "Forty
dollars an hour". Of course, lawyers can never
tell you in advance how much time they will require to settle your case. I told him that I
couldn't afford him, envisioning all the while
some astronomical legal fee like three or four
thousand dollars. He replied, "Look, I think you
are being taken for a ride because of your igno-
rance of the law. I'll take the case because I
have known you for a long time and because I like
you. Furthermore, I believe I can help. We'll
put a ceiling of five hundred dollars on it. If,
at the end of the five hundred, the case is still
dragging, I'll refer you to another, less expensive, younger attorney." I agreed. This man knew
and was known by everyone in the city's domestic
court scene. He was known and respected by the
opposing attorney. He proceeded to apply just the
right amount of pressure at the appropriate times
in the appropriate places. In brief, four hundred
and forty dollars later, I was divorced. I was
to pay neither alimony nor a cash settlement,
and I had full custody of our only child. I realized then that when an expert is operating in his
own field of endeavor and knows "where to tap the

pipe", forty dollars an hour is very inexpensive
indeed.

Recalling this episode, I took the bull by
the horns and decided that my fee would be forty
dollars an hour. I must admit that I choked or
mumbled the first few times I quoted it, but because of my credentials, I was delighted and surprised to find that no one laughed. Concomitantly,
I quoted two hundred dollars per day. I now boast
a file of letters from satisfied clients who tell
me (as I told my attorney years ago) that, in
the face of the help they derived from my work,
I am inexpensive.

But in the beginning, all was not roses.
You will discover that if you are highly recommended by another client or someone who knows you,
the prospect will never question your fee. However, if you are dealing with someone who has
never heard of you, your fee arouses suspicion.
Wanting very much to work, your first impulse
will be to lower your fee for that prospect who
is "from Missouri". Instinct told me not to, and
I didn't. Don't you ever do it either. It will
hurt your reputation and your credibility. I
learned that the questioning of the fee was just
a smokescreen for the questioning of my expertise,
since they had never heard of me. You could cut
your fee in half at this juncture, and it would
do no good. Once your credentials, your expertise

in their problem area and your general experience
are all established, there is never flak about
your fee. The client merely wants to be assured
that you can help him - - - and this is quite
reasonable. You can supply this assurance by
talking knowledgeably about similar cases in general and about his case in particular. But never
make the mistake of cutting your fees. Conversely,
never increase your fee just because you might
think that your prospective client is a "fat cat"
and that you've got him snowed. A major part of
the "credentials" I keep talking about is your
reputation, your integrity and the ethical standards you set for yourself. It is a strange psychological phenomenon, but if you know yourself
to be an ethical person and an honest one, you
will come across that way to the prospect at the
first meeting. If you know that you are a bit shady
and greedy, he will know it, too.

Now perhaps you can benefit from a big mistake that I *did* make in this matter of fees. A
prospect would call and request an exploratory
meeting with me to discuss his problems or a particular project. "Fine" I bellowed over the phone,
"my fee is forty dollars an hour." I was remem-
bering all the signs I had come across in doctors'
and dentists' offices warning that the patients
should discuss fees in advance so that there is
no embarassment later. No soap. The prospect invariably got upset with me then and there. His

general reaction went something like this: "You
expect me to pay you in order to find out whether
or not I want to do business with you? You must
be nuts." Well, this cropped up again and again
for several months, while I stupidly and stubborn-
ly stuck to my guns. Then two things dawned on
me. First, I was losing good potential business.
Second, the parallels between the consultant and
the doctor ended right there. I put myself in
the caller's place; he was right, of course.
Thereafter, I simply postponed the fee quotation
until that point in the first meeting at which
it seemed that we might work together, or until he
asked. It worked; but, more important, I worked.
Even when it didn't work, I had accomplished something almost as important; I had made another
professional contact and added that name to my
Wheeldex.

These exploratory meetings can be tricky.
From time to time, you will come across someone
who will try to use this as a "freebie" to pump
valuable information from you. He is the same
person who will attempt to discuss his gall blad-
der condition with the first physician he meets
at a cocktail party. Again the professional parallel falls apart here. The physician merely tells
this joker to make an appointment at his office
through his nurse. You, on the other hand, must
give away a few "free samples". It is the only
way to show your wares. If done deftly, he will

come away from the meeting with the full real-
ization that you have only scratched the surface
of his situation, that although impressive, the
information you gave him is worthless by itself,
and that he would do well to pay you to learn more.

Here are a few rules which now govern my
fees, and which I came to trust after painful
experience:

1. I never waive my fee - - - for anyone.
   The few times in the beginning that I
   did, I was sorry. Not placing a value
   on my time, the client considered it val-
   ueless in every instance. He therefore
   ignored whatever my input. He invariably failed in his project. And guess
   who he told everyone "helped" him with
   his project? That's right; I was the
   consultant on the job.
2. I never swap my fee or barter it for someone else's services. One party or the
   other always feels he is getting the short
   end of the stick.
3. I never work on a contingency fee basis.
   This is described in full in the next
   chapter.
4. In charging a client for expenses, I only
   charge for those expenses incurred out
   of town. I never charge him for that
   part of my office rent, my assistant's
   time, or my telephone which could be cost-

ed out to the project. I would like
to explain this, since it is my under-
standing that I am the only consultant
who works this way. Whether I had two
projects or twenty, I would maintain my
office, my phone and my assistant in any
event. It has always seemed unfair to
charge a client for any of these items.
As far as he is concerned, I could work
alone at home.

5. I have never raised my fees in ten years,
   despite the rising costs of doing business.
   Every consultant in good health is capable of working at least forty hours a
   week for fifty-two weeks out of the year.
   In my case, this would amount to a gross
   annual income of $83,200. I should like
   very much to earn this amount doing consulting work, but I don't. More important,
   I should like to work that much, because
   it's so enjoyable. So why cut down on the
   amount of work by raising the price and
   scaring a lot of small clients away?
   However, if you don't like to work, you
   shouldn't be a consultant. Come to think
   of it, you shouldn't be anything. Thinking of it further, anyone who doesn't
   like to work probably isn't anything.

VII. The Contingency Fee

VII. The Contingency Fee

The contingency fee is one which is paid to the
professional only if the project ends in success
for the client. A flat fee, on the other hand,
is paid by the client, win, lose or draw. So
all clients prefer a contingency fee. Most
professionals accept contingency fee arrangements
from time to time, depending upon the circumstances.
Except doctors. Whether the patient lives or
dies, the fee is still the same.

I am the only consultant I know who will
never accept a fee on a contingency basis. The
reasons for this are basic to the way I work and
to my fundamental attitude towards that work.

The amount of the contingency fee is invariably pegged to a percentage of the client's ultimate financial success in the project or ven-
ture. Ofttimes, however, this single project's

immediate monetary return is at odds with the long-term goals of the company or even with the success of that project itself. I am as human as the next person, which means that I like money. If I were to work on a contingency fee basis and had to advise my client to choose one of several offers regarding a project, I'm not so sure that I would elect the most beneficial one every time. I would probably point to the one with the most money involved, since that would give me the biggest fee. In another instance, I could well advise the client to take the first offer that came along, regardless of its merits, in order to conclude that project and get my fee as quickly as possible. I am, after all, selling my time.

Back to the comparison with the lawyer. A consultant has no more idea in advance of how long a project will take than does a lawyer. Things do have a way of dragging on. Not long ago, an attorney I had engaged on a contingency fee basis urged me to accept a $2500 settlement on a $72,500 lawsuit because the case had already been in negotiation for over a year and he got fed up. His fee was $750. I really felt that he hadn't served my best interests, since it was he who convinced me to sue for the original amount in the first place.

Serving the best interests of the client is

the ultimate "report card". Making a fast buck
is deleterious to your career and to your self-
esteem.

Here are two case histories which exemplify
how I work in this regard. I choose them because
in each of them, I came out on different ends
of the financial stick.

A local organization called me because it
was trying to make a business arrangement with
my former company. I was requested to go out of
town to the company headquarters, have lunch with
a vice-president who was a former co-worker of
mine, and convince her to accept the deal. I
told the client immediately that success was du-
bious in this instance due to the company's po-
licies which were adverse to his kind of propo-
sition. He insisted on retaining me to try. He
offered me $5,000 if I succeeded. I calmly quot-
ed my two-hundred-dollar-fee for the day plus
travel and luncheon expenses. He was aghast. "Man,
I'm offering you five grand for one day's work,
and you talk peanuts. How can you think so small?"
Well, my thinking went something like this: If
I accept his offer and I fail, I'm out of pocket
almost a hundred dollars; if I succeed, the fee
is unfair because no one is worth $5,000 for a
day's work. What he heard from me was simply
"Those are my fees." I was retained, I made the
pitch as best I could, and the offer was turned

down by my former colleague, as I had predicted.
I was duly paid by the client. He later tried
other means in this regard, but failed.

The second case involves a project which
reeked of success from its inception. I knew immediately what I could do and how I would do it.
Had I at that time requested one percent of the
project's eventual receipts, all the parties involved would have jumped at the offer. But I didn't.
I was retained at my daily fee. I brought the
project to a successful conclusion in two full
working days. It eventually brought the clients
$400,000 in revenues. Can't you just see my ac-
countant screaming at me in a frenzy? He did.
What kind of idiot opts for $400 instead of $4,000?
The kind of idiot who is writing this book. First
of all, no one could foretell what the ultimate
revenues would be for that project (or any other).
Second, the reason I worked so effectively is
that I was unhampered by my own possible greed.
I therefore connected smoothly and quickly with
those organizations that I knew would be most
amenable and efficient with regard to that project. I still feel good about that one. And let's
not forget the income derived from the subsequent
clients who heard about this project, and the
additional work given to me by the original client.

I remember my mother saying, when I was a
small child, "How do you know you don't want to

eat it if you don't taste it?" Yes, I tried a
contingency fee once, just to satisfy my bewil-
dered and irate accountant. Hence, my adamancy
on this subject. This is what happened.

A client came to me with a project because
he wanted me to present it to another client.
Client A offered me ten percent of the deal. I
accepted. The following day, I closed the deal.
Client B gave client A a check for $15,000. The
next day, client A sent me a check for $1,500.
Well, I thought, perhaps I have been missing the
boat after all. On the following day, client B
reconsidered and put a "stop" on the check to
client A - - - a bad practice, I agree, nevertheless he did it. I kept my fee because I had
done my part and because client A sued client B
and won. Needless to say, I lost both clients.
Had I returned the fee, it wouldn't have helped
because there was so much bad feeling all around.
Upon self-scrutinizing reflection, I realize that,
because of the contingency fee arrangement, I
behaved differently in this case than I ever have
before or since. I had taken this project to the
first people I knew would jump at it, particularly if they thought it was a bargain. I had
also concluded the deal at the first and lowest
offer. I did not deliberate whether it was in
the best interests of the project itself to put
these two clients together. The fact that client
B had second thoughts after I left his office

bears all of this out. In truth, I saw a fast
$1,500 flashing in neon lights before my eyes
during this entire matter. I don't know; maybe
I shouldn't have kept the fee after all.

I am convinced that whatever good reputation I have is partially based on the fact that
I do not accept contingency fee arrangements.

VIII. Money

VIII. Money

Here is a picture of my gross receipts for the
first five years of my free lancing and consulting. This is on a calendar-year basis. I started
in the Spring of 1967.

1967	$ 9,000.
1968	$22,000.
1969	$33,000.
1970	$46,000.
1971	$51,000.

Simple figuring of inflation will transform these
amounts to today's values.

When I left the employ of my former firm,
I was earning $16,000 a year, including bonuses.
One must also consider the many tax advantages
of being self-employed. There are absolutely none
while working for someone else, as you well know.

The curve did not continue to rise in the

same manner for the next five years, as far as
my consulting work was concerned. I was, however,
in a position to take financial part in several
ventures in my industry to which I was exposed
in my capacity as consultant, and I was quick
to seize the opportunities. My position in these
matters gave me the inside track, so to speak,
and I was able to make fairly intelligent decisions in this regard.

Imagine, after four years, being able to
earn as much money free lancing and consulting
in your own field as any United States Senator
or Congressman, with none of the hassles and in
a much more gratifying way. Well, that is really
coming up in the world. I am not shy about crow-
ing a bit here, and you won't be either when it
happens to you.

In the third year, I found that I could not
sustain the work load alone, and I hired an assistant. I use the word "assistant" advisedly, because
I did not then, and do not now need a secretary.
I find that it takes twice as much time to dictate a letter to a secretary and have her type
it as it does to sit down at a typewriter myself
and complete the letter in one motion. My right
index finger is not arthritic, so I am also perfect-
ly capable of dialing the telephone myself. Besides, I cannot abide the ludicrous game that
secretaries play with each other to the tune of

"Put your Mr. X on, and then I'll put my Mr. Y on." And here again, I have never lost any "image" by answering my own phone or not having secretarial initials on the bottom of my letters.

After much interviewing, I decided on someone who had never worked in the business world before and hence hadn't picked up any bad working habits. I wanted a *tabula rasa*, so I hired a young lady fresh out of graduate school, who commended herself to me by dint of the facts that: she came from a fine family, she had a good working knowledge of the English language, and although she could type only slowly she could proof-read her own work accurately and was somewhat of a perfectionist. She also had an excellent telephone voice. Most of all, she was intelligent, trustworthy, eager, and a rapid learner. Her starting salary was $5,200 a year. Within two years, she was earning fifty percent more than that. Within four years, her salary was almost doubled.

My assistant's work consisted mainly of back-up details: a certain amount of bookkeeping, the handling of the mail, and the knowledgeable running of the office when I was out of town. She was always totally aware of everything that went on in the office. The main reason for this was my having had the dividing wall torn down two years before. She was privy to every conversation, phone call and written communication. In short

order, the clients came to know and trust her.
She is no longer in my employ because, unfortu-
nately, a consultant's assistant is not an assistant consultant. No client would seek or pay for
her advice. So it was a dead-end job, and she
ultimately resigned.

But, back to money. There are two ways to
have it. One way is to earn it. The other way
is not to spend it. If you can do both, you will
wind up with twice as much. I was earning enough
to buy an expensive car (I use my car often for
business), to move my office into the fashionable
end of town, to install expensive furniture and
equipment, and even to hire a second person. I
was advised that the Internal Revenue Service
would actually be paying for a goodly percentage
of all this anyway. But I neither needed nor had
any desire for any of those things. I liked my
old car; we had become friends. Certainly there
was no new building in the swank section of town
which allowed me the privilege of opening or
closing a window or turning on the air-conditioner
on a hot off-season day, much less bringing my
dog to work. And one with a real fireplace? I
was comfortable in my office as it was. As for
an additional employee, I use a "temporary" on
the few occasions when the work load is that heavy.
To the contrary, I kept heading in the other di-
rection; when I costed out the Xerox machine I
had rented against individual copies at the in-

stant print shop downstairs, I returned the machine. Superfluity of any kind is wasteful.

Elizabeth Seton once advised "Live simply so that others may simply live." That is both true and noble. But my working life is kept simple so that *I* may simply live another day. My income is neither guaranteed nor steady. Nor is my good health assured forever. Not spending profligately nor taxing my small business inordinately because of personal desires for needless luxuries gives me the ultimate luxury: peace of mind and the assurance that I will always have an office. Besides, the Internal Revenue Service actually pays for nothing. It would be my fellow citizens who would be paying for my impetuousness - - - and that's not fair.

A word about temporary help. Employment agencies that specialize in this kind of work are amazingly good, as a general rule. They are uncanny in the way that they rate and categorize their people. For a low hourly fee, you will get a fairly dull, but conscientious unskilled person. For twice that amount, you will get one of the brightest, skilled and capable people you ever came across. This is someone who cannot abide the humdrum life of going to the same office and doing the same things all of her life, but thrives on diversity. Then you have all the accurate gradations in between. All, however, are eager and

willing to work, and I have never known any to
take possible advantage of the temporary employer. Most important, there is absolutely no waste.
The very moment the job is completed, the person
is dismissed and you stop paying.

I am probably representing myself as Scrooge
incarnate. That is only part of the picture. I
do let loose the financial reins in some aspects
of my work, i.e. business lunches and other forms
of business entertainment, business trips not paid
for by clients but which might possibly bring me
into contact with prospective clients, and long-
distance telelphone calls. Indeed, anything that
will open the lines of communication between my
office and the outside world, I find worth spending for.

Approximately two-fifths of my annual revenue
is spent on the cost of doing business as a consultant. This puts me into a fairly high tax
bracket for a little guy. But, after paying Uncle
Sam, I find that I have more than enough left to
live very well by any standards, and still have
"a little something" left over.

Most important, I have no debts. I pay all
of my bills on the day that I receive them. Try
that sometime for peace of mind. Conversely, I
bill all clients within two days after the service
is performed for them. I then meticulously follow

up all my invoices with monthly statements and
phone calls. Since I have been both flat broke
and comparatively well off in a short period of
time, I am very comfortable about money and
have absolutely no embarrassment about asking
for it from anyone who owes it to me for an
undue length of time. Money just isn't a
dirty word in my vocabulary. As a result, out
of a total billing for ten years of over $400,000,
I have collected all except $40 - - - and I would
have gotten to that dead-beat if he hadn't skip-
ped to California. My accountant is incredulous
and assures me that this must be some kind of all-
time world record. Maybe it is.

IX. Consulting, At Last

IX. Consulting, At Last

It was exactly ten months after I had set myself up, established my hourly fee and had been working on long-term projects for monthly retainers, that I started abruptly to do actual consulting. I received three telephone inquiries within one week. Two of them were from individuals who had found my name in the Yellow Pages. The third was from the executive director of a large organization; he had heard about me from someone I had never met (this has happened a number of times). In all three cases, I asked them to identify the general nature of their problems on the phone and apprised them of my hourly fee. All confirmed appointments for three different days.

A word about those Yellow Pages. I have never placed an advertisement in them. I simply have the regular listing to which I am entitled by dint of the fact that I have a phone. Over the

years, I have averaged one inquiry per week from
this source.

I must confess that, unbeknownst to the client,
I experienced extreme "stage fright" before each
of these meetings. They didn't know that they were
my first; this was certainly nothing to advertise.
What would they ask? What vast stores of knowledge
was I supposed to be the repository of? What if
their problems dealt with subjects and areas I
had never been exposed to? What, in short, if I
didn't have the answers? Forty dollars an hour!
Big shot! Now I was on the proverbial spot. What
do I do if they ask ten questions and I can only
answer five? Give them back twenty dollars? How
many people in what short period of time would
they tell that I was a fraud?

Well, my friend was right, of course. We
don't know how much we know. The sessions went
smoothly and professionally. Without any specific preparation (impossible, because I didn't
know the actual questions in advance), I was both
knowledgeable and erudite in every instance. The
clients were pleasantly surprised at the amount
of useful information they received in one hour's
time. No, I didn't stretch it out to increase
my fee. I had something to prove to them and to
myself - - - that I was a bargain. And I did.

This "stage fright" did not end after those

three sessions. It cropped up again and again
for two more years. Not always. Just in those
instances where I had forgotten how much experience I really had. Always, this uneasiness left
me within the first five minutes of the consul-
tation.

So, above my regular income that first week,
I earned another $120 for three hours of work.
The most pleasant and exhilarating work I had
ever done. A taste of blood, so to speak. I wanted more, much more of this. I realized, though,
that, just like those first three, the rest would
have to come in of its own accord. There was nothing I could do to push it, rush it or in any
way make it happen. The only thing I did was carefully add those three names to my Wheeldex. Over
the years, I have sent these people and those
who followed, some unusual communication at Christ-
mastime to remind them that I am still here should
they ever need me.

I did one thing, however, which helped me
as I went along. I printed up a partial list of
clients on my stationery. Partial because I only
listed the more familiar and notable names. As
the list grew, so did my credibility as a consultant with prospective clients. Now, whenever I
presented my calling card, I also proffered my
list. I have the list reprinted and lengthened
every six months.

CONSULTING, AT LAST

My consultancy started to pyramid. With that, my reputation pyramided, too. Requests started to trickle in for me to speak about my industry before small groups. At first, I jumped at the chance to do this free of charge. Later, as the groups became larger, I required an honorarium. Additional requests came in for me to write articles in trade publications. Here again, I started without benefit of fee and later charged for it. The Mark Twain syndrome was repeating itself, in a sense.

All of this activity brought the yearned-for additional consulting work. Two years after those first phone calls, my consulting work accounted for fifty percent of my revenue. I had arrived.

X. Contracts

X. Contracts

I am the only consultant I ever heard of who absolutely refuses to enter into any legal contractual agreement with a client. As a consequence,
this cannot be a chapter on how to write an air-
tight contract. Rather, I would hope to make you
understand why I shun them. Perhaps I can convince you to do likewise.

It is most often the consultant who tries
to get the client to sign a contract, not the
other way around. The client is usually shy of
this. What if the consultant doesn't produce,
proves himself inept somewhere down the line,
becomes lazy, misses meetings or writes an un-
intelligible final report? The client would be
stuck. So, pragmatically, pushing a contract into a client's face and trying to force him to
use legal counsel to make a deal with you simply
cuts your chances of working in half.

CONTRACTS

Let us assume, however, that a one-year contract is signed by the client, engaging your services. You are now married to each other. The first
two months comprise the honeymoon. You are the
darling of the company. Everyone is running around,
pointing you out as the genius who is going to
solve all of their problems, eliminate their competition, and make them a huge success. After
all, they have a contract. Let us even assume that
you are indeed good enough to accomplish this
inane one-year goal. It will take you some time,
even though you are a genius, to get started.
It takes a couple of months just to get acquainted
with how they have been doing things wrong. Their
middle management will be constantly trying to
hide it from you. You bill them monthly, because
this is the usual procedure and the only sensible
one. By the end of the third month, they still
haven't conquered the world and they see no tangible progress. A bit of the heartiness goes out
of their greeting in the morning. You are not
slapped quite so hard on the back anymore. You
are invited to fewer meetings. They become somewhat soured by the fact that your monthly invoices
are going to be arriving like clockwork for the
next nine months, and as yet they have nothing
concrete to show for their payments. They are
finding it just a bit difficult to justify your
presence and your expense to their comptroller.
In short, the honeymoon is over. You are stuck
with each other. You are grudgingly going to their

meetings, and they are grudgingly paying your invoices. The relationship should terminate right here, but it can't. There is a contract, and the first one to even suggest termination is "in breach". Then it becomes bitter. They may lose some more money, but you lose reputation - - - and the work is no longer enjoyable.

Here is another reason to eschew contracts. A consultant is not a TV repairman. The work is neither that precise nor that cut-and-dried. But even a TV repairman will not quote a price for his work until he sees exactly what is wrong with the set. You do not have that opportunity on any long-range project. You go into a contractual agreement with absolutely no idea of how much of your time it will take, what political obstacles you will meet, how many meetings a week your client will require you to attend, and what tangential business of theirs you must familiarize yourself with to accomplish their goals. Your retainer is only a wild guess on your part. You could well be required to put in so much time, that you come out having earned an average of $3.50 an hour by the end of the year or whatever the contractual period. Without a contract, the fee may be renegotiated anywhere along the line by either party, up or down. The consultant/client relationship has a much better chance of thriving.

Again, suppose you start working and find

that your client is involved in practices that
are against your moral principles. If you signed
a contract, you are stuck.

It has always seemed to me that contracts
are entrapments. Remember, you chose the career
of consulting to avoid being trapped in life
ever again. Now you are back where you started.
Let's return to the professional parallel with
the doctor, dentist, or psychiatrist. No property
is being negotiated here, just as in your case.
If one person needs help and the other person
is willing and capable of giving it, who needs
lawyers, legal contracts and their attendant expense? If a prospective client insists on it,
I automatically don't trust him. The only time
it is ever necessary to sign a contract is when
you do work for any government agency on a long-
term project. For me this is a moot point, because I make it a practice never to deal with
government this way (more about that later).

With regard to long-term or ongoing projects,
here is what I do. I always request, and get,
a letter of intent from the individual client
or responsible executive representing an organization. In this letter is a general description
of the work required of me and the monthly fee to
be paid. There is also a sentence which states
that either party may terminate this arrangement
with thirty days of prior notice to the other.

Prospects are very pleasantly surprised to come upon such an arrangement. When I proffer it, they look upon me as being guileless, which I am. They are also more easily able to enter into such an agreement because it does not require a large-figure entry into the annual budget beforehand, and therefore doesn't require approval from a superior, comptroller, or board of directors. Recall that my very first client retained me for over six years on this basis.

The strangest and nicest thing about this kind of letter of intent is that it is, in effect, legally binding. I had an unfortunate incident in which this legality was tested. Here is what happened.

One of the largest professional associations in the country called upon me to do a study concerning the feasibility of a project. My study proved the project feasible. The executive in charge of the division called me in and asked if I would like to administer the project on a free-lance basis. I agreed. I then quoted my fee for the project. He accepted with the proviso that I waive my bill for the feasibility study. I agreed to this, too, because I liked both the man and his project. I requested my usual letter of intent setting all of this forth on one page in simple language. The letter arrived the following day, and I immediately started work. Se-

CONTRACTS

veral weeks later, this man was promoted to another division, and another man moved into his
place. This second individual called me into his
office, thanked me for what I had done, and informed me that the association could very well
proceed without me. I quickly turned the letter
of intent over to my attorney, who sued forthwith on the strength of that letter. The matter
was settled out of court, and the association
paid me $10,000.

I rest my case concerning contracts.

XI. The Work

XI. The Work

A consultant's work is so wondrously varied that
it would be impossible to categorize or describe
the assignments that have come to me and will
possibly come to you. However, since "the impossible only takes a little longer" I shall attempt
it.

You will be asked how to accomplish any task
in any facet of your industry in the most expedi-
tious and economical way. Thereafter, you may be
asked to actually do the work itself. If you demur
on the second part, you are an ivory-tower-beard-
stroking consultant. If not, you are a working
consultant. The working consultant is usually
busier, earns more money (it's the same hourly
fee whether you work or talk), gains a better
reputation faster, and has the confidence of the
client by dint of the fact that he is willing to

put into practice what he preached rather than pontificate and run.

You will be asked for pure, hard, current information dealing with your profession or industry. You must either have this information in your head or be familiar with the referential sources from which you can glean it. These sources may repose in an extensive library in your office or in the public library, or both. Your primary requisite for this kind of consulting is the careful reading of every respected trade or professional publication in your field. Your clients generally don't have the time to do this. You must make the time.

There is a big secondary benefit to extensive and thorough trade or professional reading. It will save you lots of time and money; remember that time and money are one and the same in your work. You will get a complete overview plus all the "meat" of any seminar, lecture or convention you thought you might attend for your own educational purposes. Ofttimes the concepts will present themselves more clearly by reading about them in your chosen surroundings than by actually attending these meetings. Seminars, meetings and conventions are obscured and obfuscated by booze, hullabaloo, stupid questions, fatigue and agenda items which insult your itelligence and experience. Of course, if you just want to take a tax-deductible trip to get away from it all, that is a different matter. Also, good contacts can sometimes be made at conventions to which prospective clients in your field may throng. Generally, however, you can accomplish more for yourself and for your clients by staying home and "tending your garden", reading all the while. Once in a while, you may be asked to attend a convention in your client's behalf for your regular fee; that is a convention not to be missed.

You will be asked to make a pitch or present a deal for a client. Why doesn't he use one of his salesmen or do it himself? Because he is smart. You are an independent. Coming from you, the deal has more credibility and sincerity. Besides, the one to be pitched to may be another of your clients or just someone in the field who has confidence in you.

You will be asked to do a feasibility study on a project which the client would like to embark upon but wants outside reassurance. Conversely, you will be asked to do a similar study because a client does *not* want to take a particular course of action and wants to present an unbiased, independent report to his board of directors; he wants this report to tell them that the project in question is foolhardy and the executive in charge is not merely lazy. In either case, never accept an assignment in which the client tells you beforehand the conclusions he wants. It may force you to fudge and lie - - - a detriment to your reputation and integrity.

You will be asked to recommend a candidate to fill a sensitive job opening. Conversely, you will be asked if you know of any job opportunities. Be careful here. Never recommend either way, unless you know that the job is suited to the person and *vice versa*. Again, your reputation is on the line. Never accept or request a fee for this service. If you are able to handle this kind of request expertly and to the satisfaction of both parties, your reward will come in the form of consulting work from this quarter further down the line, out of respect and gratitude.

You will be asked to sit in on a brainstorming session just because you have a good mind and because you are objective. The purpose here is to have you come up with some ideas that the other attendees may miss because they are too close to the situation and "cannot see the forest for the trees".

You will be asked to carry out a job or a chore that the client thought up but is too lazy to do himself. An exaggerated, ludicrous, but true example is the time a client paid me forty dollars an hour to take a bunch of mail to the post office and have each piece registered.

Getting to the periphery of this subject, if your client is located out of town, you may be asked to entertain a V.I.P. while he or she is in your city.

Finally, you will be asked to write reports about everything: feasibility studies, progress, regress, methodology, budgets, what you think, what your client thinks, the state of the industry, and personnel evaluation. You should be able to write concisely and clearly in an organized way with a good command of the language.

Believe it or not, all of the above will take up about half of your time. But don't be idle, ever. The other half of the time is where the creative part comes in. I am one of the few consultants in the country (or possibly the world) who works the way that I do in the second half. Indeed, I regard the first half as subsidy to allow me to devote myself to the second.

Surely, by this time, I have revealed quite a bit of myself in this book. If you haven't as yet picked up on the fact that I am a highly energized, self-motivated, cerebral individual, you either haven't been reading attentively or I don't know how to communicate with you.

It isn't just that I never stop thinking. It's that I never stop doing. Doing what? Doing

what I think about. You have heard the expression
"Ideas are a dime a dozen". Not true. Ideas are
a nickel a gross. Ideas, in fact, are worthless
unless someone does something about them. Most
of us, at one time or another, have asked "Why
don't they do something about _____?"
Who are "they"? Why don't *you*? Well, that is what
I do with the other half of my time. I'm constantly musing about how my industry can be improved,
and continuously trying to come up with ways to
make those improvements happen. Whenever I get
an idea that seems sound, I pick up the phone and
call a respected executive with clout, make an
appointment and tell him my idea. Almost everyone
will talk with a consultant. By the way, I am
not anal retentive about these ideas; as we discovered, by themselves, they are worthless any-
how. At this point, one of several things will
happen:

  a) The man across the desk will clap me on
     the back, tell me that I am a genius,
     adopt or adapt the idea for his firm and
     dismiss me. Always remember, *no one pays
     for unrequested ideas.* Or
  b) He will accept the idea and ask me to carry
     it out for him for a fee. Or
  c) He will tell me that my brainchild is un-
     workable and give me sixteen good reasons
     why. Whereupon, I will either fold my tent,
     or go back to the drawing board. Or
  d) He will reinforce my idea but tell me that

he is just too lazy (stupid) or too busy
(stupid) to do anything about it.

If it is "d" and my idea requires a fair-sized
investment of capital, I'll take it to others who
are not stupid. If it doesn't require much money,
but only a whole lot of work, I will immediately
set about doing it myself. After all, I have the
time (which equates to money), the know-how and
the contacts.

Let me cite two examples of how this has
worked for me. It is worth taking the time to
go into this in some detail because this is the
creative, innovative area of consulting work that
you don't normally read or hear about.

One evening in 1970, I was sitting in the
theatre waiting for the curtain to rise, when
something caught my eye in the program/magazine,
"Why don't they_____?" I thought. The
next morning I telephoned the executive vice-
president of the company in question. He listened for a few minutes and invited me to come and
visit him. When I arrived, he dismissed my idea
forthwith explaining that he had tried that a
few years before and it hadn't worked. But he
was intrigued by my phone call because "great
minds run in the same track", as he put it (he
was obviously as big an egotist as I), because
of my assertiveness or *chutzpah* in calling him

personally, and because of some "mystical force" which had me call just when he was seeking the services of a consultant in my field regarding a different matter. I was retained for three months at a fee of $500 a month to accomplish his task. The job was done in two months.

One year later, I was lying on the beach at Nags Head, North Carolina, and an idea for a totally unique marketing method came to me. I spoke with five different company principals about it. Mind you, I was *giving* it away. I just wanted to see it done. All were enthused, but none would do anything about it. I sold a few acres of country property I had acquired two years before. Armed with this money, my marketing scheme, and the previous enthusiasm of my do-nothing colleagues, I set up a small company to do it myself. Within six months, the plan netted $22,000. I was satisfied. It worked. That is all I really cared about. I did not want to be a businessman and give up my life of freedom. I went to one of my clients and sold the business for $75,000.

I am still doing this kind of thing. Not all of my ideas are workable. The point is that whenever I get an idea, I concomitantly have a surging need to know whether or not it will work. I keep a file called "ideas". I fully intend to prove or disprove every one of them before I die.

I have one other method of accumulating work. Whenever I plan a trip anywhere over two thousand miles, whether on vacation, in my own professional behalf, or on assignment for a client, I send a letter to all of my clients informing them of this. In this letter, I ask if there is any task or errand they would like me to attend to for them in that faraway place. Invariably, I get some response. You see, the client immediately realizes that the biggest expenses - - - fare, hotels and meals - - - are already paid for. If he has something to be done in that distant city which would take only two hours, it will only cost him eighty dollars. It certainly doesn't pay for him to send one of his people or go himself at those rates. You would be surprised at how many of my trips have been subsidized in this manner. Do these odd jobs put a crimp in my trip? Not at all. You forget; I love my work.

Time and again, a client who is impressed with your work and your know-how, will offer you a lucrative, full-time executive position in his company. These offers are tempting, but you will have to muster all of your will power and refuse them. Otherwise, you will lose your hard-won freedom. Besides, you would not be nearly as effective back in the table of organization as you are now in your independent state. Your job-offering client doesn't realize this, but you must.

XII. Ethics and Practices

XII. Ethics and Practices

Since consultants are neither organized nor li-
censed, there is no fixed code of ethics and no
set of rules and regulations they must conform
to. On one level, each person pretty much adheres
to his or her own moral strictures. On this subject, a funny story comes to mind.

A ten-year old boy was doing his homework
while his father sat in the same room, reading
his newspaper. The boy looked up and asked, "Dad,
what does 'ethics' mean?" The father put down
his paper and explained carefully as follows:
"Well, you know that sometimes my customers leave
things accidentally in the pockets of the clothing
they bring into my dry-cleaning store. Suppose,
after a customer leaves the shop, I find a ten-
dollar bill in one of his pockets. Here is where
'ethics' enters into the situation. The question
immediately arises as to whether or not I should

tell my partner."

It is not for me to tell you how to comport yourself in your newly chosen profession. I can only pass on my own ten commandments (I sometimes liken myself to Moses) to which I have conformed without strain over the years, and which may have had something to do with my successful relationships with my clients.

I. Thou shalt always work to the best of thine ability to ensure the quick success of thy client's project.

II. Thou shalt not waive, lower or raise thy hourly or daily fee for any one particular client.

III. Thou shalt not become involved in thy client's organizational politics.

IV. Thou shalt not accept the assignment of any fee for personnel placement.

V. Thou shalt not be idle.

VI. Thou shalt never "load" time or an expense account.

VII. Thou shalt not accept the assignment of any study or investigation which has a forgone conclusion by the client.

VIII. Thou shalt not lie to a client.

IX. Thou shalt not accept a contingency fee.

X. Thou shalt not quit by accepting a full-time position and becoming an employee once again.

How you practice your consultancy will turn out to be a very individual thing according to some of your already ingrained work habits and attitudes. But here is a description of some of my methods, should you find them useful.

Without sacrificing thoroughness, I always work as fast and as soon as possible. Getting an assignment completed quickly frees me to accept other assignments without time conflicts. Juggling four assignments at once sometimes boggles the mind. As a result, my desk is usually cleared when the next call comes through and I can give the client my undivided attention. (This backfired on me once when a new client noted the neat appearance of my desk. I quoted the old adage "A cluttered desk portrays a cluttered mind". He replied, "That's true. What worries me is that your desk is empty.") If a piece of work is due six weeks hence, I apply myself to it in such a concentrated way that I generally turn it in three weeks early. I also begin work immediately, even though I may have enough time to start work later, because I like to start when the problem is fresh in my mind. My clientele seems to appreciate this methodology.

I always come right to the point. Although I am never abrupt when establishing a rapport with a client while attempting to discover his true goals, I am extremely blunt and border on

abrasiveness when dealing with the actual problems and tasks. It has always seemed to me that
deep down the client appreciates this kind of
incisive candor when paying by the hour. Friends,
relations or employees of the client may all have
their own emotional and/or tangible reasons for
telling him what he wants to hear, but my function
as consultant is entirely different. For example,
I have often told individual clients who have
brought me samples of their work with a need for
professional evaluation that they have absolutely no talent in this area and that they are wast-
ing their time and money; I have recommended that
they either give it up or go to school. I can also be just as candid in the opposite case, and
urge the talented individual on with much more
than encouragement. Indeed, I will pick up the
phone and immediately put that client in touch
with important contacts in the industry.

Another example. An attorney once called
to enlist my services. Knowing nothing about my
industry, he wanted to invest money in it by
opening a place of business and hiring an experienced manager. He was about to sign a long-term
lease and wanted my opinion about the location.
The site was fifty miles from my office, so it
was necessary to book him in advance for a full
day's work. I deliberately arrived in my car one
hour early so that I could drive around and apprise
myself of the territory before we met. The pros-

pects, from every point of view, were dismal.
At the appointed time, I told him of my find-
ings in no uncertain terms. It took all of ten
minutes. I got back into my car and somewhat a-
bashedly told him that I would have to bill him
for $200, my daily fee. His rejoinder was, "Hell,
that's the best $200 I ever spent. You just saved
me over $30,000 on a lease that would have been
worthless to me. I am grateful." Of course, that
was one of my more intelligent clients. Regardless
of the client's attributes, I always work the
same way.

I draw no line when it comes to blunt advice.
I have told the owner of a small business that
was suffering from internal theft that his brother-
in-law was stealing him blind. I have told the
president of a large business that his **general**
manager was totally incompetent and was the cause
of the loss of a number of high-calibre junior
executives. I have told a client that there ought
to be a law against what he was doing. I have
told a client that his work was so good that I
could guarantee his selling one piece of it for
a minimum of $5,000 (he did).

About half of my clients don't take my advice. Those that do, take only half of the advice.
But you will not be paid on the basis of whether
or not your advice is taken. You will be paid
for advice given. A great number of people make

appointments with consultants for strange and
even bizarre reasons, most of which they themselves are not aware of. Some of them either have
a need for or will confuse you with a psychiatrist. They will enter your office, talk freely
and constantly for one hour, and leave happily
without your having said a word. This is obviously some kind of catharsis for them, and they have
no one else they can speak to in a confidential
atmosphere. Some clients will use you as a sound-
ing board for their ideas; whether you agree or
disagree with them, they act on those ideas any-
how. Some clients want to plunge ahead with high-
priced, high-risk investment schemes. I always
advise testing the plan first, and they ofttimes
become annoyed with me. Some clients have a com-
pulsive need to lose large amounts of money; I
advise them to join Gambler's Anonymous.

Finally, I never take on any assignment
which shows every sign of failure and no chance
of success. I like winners, not losers.

I wouldn't exactly call these practices techniques. Rather, they are manifestations of who I
am. Who you are will dictate your practices and
your ethics. After all, you are becoming a consultant to "do your own thing".

XIII. Competition

XIII. Competition

There is virtually no competition in consulting.
Once again, the comparison with the other professions is very close. Each doctor, lawyer, and
accountant builds his own clientele. None, to my
knowledge, solicit their colleagues' clients.
After a while, each gains his or her own reputation which attracts new clients or patients.

There are basically three types of consultants: the independent (you and I), the influence
peddler, whom we have discussed earlier in this
book, and the large management consulting firm.

In the beginning, I must confess to a certain amount of awe concerning the large firm which
is incorporated with a zillion names on the door
and letterhead. How could I possibly compete with
or stand up to them? Their names are like house-
hold words and their offices look like banks.

COMPETITION

Recall, if you will, those first three calls I received for purely consultative work many years ago. One of them was from a large organization. On my first visit, the executive in charge opened the meeting by tossing a weighty report across the desk at me. It was eighty pages long and most handsomely (and expensively) bound. The name of the esteemed consulting firm embossed in gold leaf on the cover made me gasp. This was my very first major consulting assignment. Surely no one expected me to stand alongside, let alone be in the same ballpark, with *them*! I looked up, and the client, his face purple with rage, threw three words at me: "Read that horseshit." He then went on to tell me that the eminent consulting firm sent in "some young snotnose with a newly minted master's degree in business administration from Harvard" who had nothing to recommend him but an expensive necktie and an attaché case which was the talk of the office complex. Three weeks later, the firm presented my client with a bill for $3,000 and the report which I held in my hands. The report was a perfect example of an unprepared high-school student's attempt to puff up a paper about a book he had never read. In it, eighty pages were devoted to defining the problem, complete with a table of contents and index. "Dammit", yelled my client, "I know the problem. I know it well enough to try to get some help around here. I need some solutions." I felt on much firmer ground then.

I offered to tackle the job and complete it
in one working week for $700. I went to work on
the following day. I was there four hours, when
I recognized the impasse. The middle-management
executive in charge, who was assigned to assist
me in gathering the data and information I required, was a total incompetent. He had obviously covered his tracks and fooled my predecessor.
He had kept no records in his division for five
years and had instructed his clerical staff to
do likewise. There were no sales records, no
packing slips, and no invoices. All that remained
were bookkeeping records in the ledger books in
the comptroller's office. I quickly assessed the
cost to management of writing to all its resources
requesting duplicate documents and reconstructing
the whole picture. At three o'clock, I asked to
see my client in private. I explained what I had
found, why it would not pay him to put the pieces
of the puzzle together, and why I could not give
him the answers he wanted. I was careful not to
mention the other consulting firm. I strongly recommended that he immediately dismiss his division
head for either incompetence or the cover-up of
something more serious. I told him that, although
I had set the week aside for him, it would not
be fair to charge him the full fee, since I could
not fulfill my original function. I would put into
writing what I had found and simply charge him
$200, my daily fee. It was immediately apparent
to him, as it had been to me all day long, that

127

the prestigious consulting firm had taken him for
a long ride by stretching this futile situation
into a three-week project and filing the nonsensical report. One month later, this client called
me back and retained me at $800 per month to ad-
minister that division on a free-lance basis. I
worked on that project for one year and put the
section back on its feet.

Since then, I have never worried about competition from the behemoths of the profession.
The bigger they are, the less functional. Small
is beautiful. The bigger they are, the higher
their prices and the better my chances with my
fees. Some companies, which are highly specialized,
are effective. But those which claim to be able
to solve all problems in all fields under the
guise of "management" are pulling the wool over
sleeping eyes. Lots of luck to them.

You will have no competition.

XIV. Case History

XIV. Case History

Sometimes, in an expository book like this, it is necessary to concoct a case history which incorporates at least one example of every rule and theory previously set forth. I think we are more fortunate, because I truly worked for one particular client on a big project which ideally exemplifies the main themes of almost every chapter. I have only changed the names to preserve the confidentiality that my profession requires. Everything else is written exactly as it happened and nothing is contrived.

To give you the total picture, let's begin at the very beginning. Two weeks after my fir assistant came to work for me, she was still trying to sort out and familiarize herself with the many facets of my work. So she was further taxed one morning when I announced that on the following day, and for the next weeks, she would be re-

quired to assist me at the annual convention of
my trade association. I explained that the association itself was my client and that each year
I helped them at their convention with their displays and their seminars. On the second day of
the meeting, I was required to sit on the speak-
er's dais during the official luncheon. My assistant sat, unescorted, at one of the tables.
During lunch, a gentleman on her right struck
up a conversation with her. He began in the usual
manner at such functions by asking about her name-
tag. Whom did she work for, what did an assistant
to a consultant do, and what kind of work did the
consultant himself do? The young lady could only
blurt out that she was completely overwhelmed
by the industry, by the convention and by the
past two and one-half weeks. She said that nothing,
as yet, had come together for her, but that the
man she worked for seemed to be nice and very
competent in his work. This candor obviously struck
some kind of chord, because Mr. Bianco presented
her with his card, told her that his firm was a-
bout to embark on a huge undertaking, and asked
that I telephone him as soon as the convention
was over. My assistant could not know then that
Mr. Bianco was vice-president of the largest company in the industry.

I wasted no time in calling and setting up
the appointment. The meeting lasted two hours,
and I did not charge for this exploratory time.

I learned that the company was building a new
edifice which would cost over $125,000,000. A
very small division would be expanded in this
new building. Would I give the architects the
benefit of my experience from a commercial point
of view concerning this one part of the building?
Would I also plan the new budget, the staff and
the inventory, offer innovative ideas, and help
the manager to adjust smoothly to his new operation? This was a wonderful opportunity for me.
I agreed to start work at my forty-dollar-an-hour
fee. Mr. Bianco introduced me to Mr. Packer, the
manager of the division in question. Mr. Packer
and I went to lunch and hit it off well. I was
particularly impressed with his devotion to the
company. He had been working there for fifteen
years and knew what he was about.

At this juncture, let me explain that in
any long-term ongoing project, the consultant
works the most assiduously and intensely in the
very beginning, particularly in a situation of
this kind which calls for simultaneous endeavor
with many different people in many different divisions. After the first couple of months, if
he has done well, most of the divisions are working synergistically on his plans and recommenda-
tions, the work is carried on in a more relaxed
atmosphere, and his time on the job is spread
out more evenly. So my bill to the client for
the first month was somewhat steep because of

the large chunk of concentrated time I had devoted initially to the project. With the payment of the bill came a phone call from the vice-president. He told me that the president wanted to see me.

Mr. Bianco ushered me into the office and the president greeted me warmly. We had met perfunctorily on several previous occasions. He told me that he was very pleased with my work thus far and that he was certain that, with my help, the project would be a huge success. In fact, he wanted the first year's operation budgeted at two million dollars (an astounding sum). "But very frankly, Hubert" he went on "your forty-dollar-an-hour fee is making me nervous because it is open-ended and we don't know how to budget for it. I would feel much more comfortable with a flat fee for the entire job." It took me a while to believe what I had just heard from this multi-millionaire whose family name would grace the facade of a new building costing more than Dulles International Airport. But maybe, I thought, that was one of his functions as president. I watched my pennies; why shouldn't he? I decided not to take umbrage. I told him that I could quote a flat fee, but that he would have to guarantee that the new division would be operational by a given date. He answered that he couldn't one hundred percent guarantee it, but that he was fairly certain it would be open by the following July. On that basis, I demurred, but count-

ered with a monthly retainer of $700. This he
accepted gladly, we shook hands on it, and I
received my letter of intent from Mr. Bianco
to this effect two days later. The new place
became operational two years after that, so I
had decided correctly in my own behalf. The president, however, had erred in his judgment because the entire project would have cost him less
on an hourly basis, as it turned out.

My first big task, as I saw it, was to figure out how this proposed plant, bursting new-
born upon society as it would, could possibly
take in two million dollars in its first year.
I came up with an entirely new and different mer-
chandising scheme which I believed to be a fool-
proof way of attracting the public's attention.
It was rejected. They meant to do it in the tra-
ditional way. How, I could never glean from them.
I was to budget on that basis. Shouln't we have
an alternate, lower budget, just in case? No. I
don't have to tell you that they didn't approach
the two million in the first year. Nevertheless,
I budgeted their way.

By this time, Mr. Packer and I had been working closely and consistently together. I was impressed with his knowledge and his experience as
well as with the fine relationship he seemed to
enjoy with his employees and fellow workers. He
paved the way for me in many areas of my work,

thereby cutting down on my time and making things
smoother all around. The only thing that distres-
sed me about him was that he was having a difficult time adjusting conceptually to the scope of
the newly planned operation which would be gar-
gantuan in size, compared to the one he was now
running. For example, to accommodate that much
business, it was necessary for me to budget a
minimum payroll of thirty employees. "What will
I do with that many people?" he asked. In fact,
thirty could barely accomplish the work, but he
couldn't fathom it.

At the end of one year, my work had come to
an end. It merely remained for them to carry out
everything that had been planned. As I said before, this took another year, what with labor
strikes and other delays. Mr. Bianco called me
into his office to thank me for what I had done,
and gave me one final assignment. Would I send
him a written evaluative report on Mr. Packer's
chances of succeeding as manager of this new endeavor, based on my close-hand observation of
him for one year? I had mixed feelings about this,
to say the least. On the one hand, I felt that
I had been retained in part to spy on one of their
people, and this was distasteful to me. On the
other hand, I felt that this request was only
meet and proper for the success of the new division. Since success is always the original and
ultimate goal, I filed my report.

I wrote that Mr. Packer was a very valuable
employee to the corporation and described in detail all of his fine attributes. I also gave full
credit for his assistance to me in my work. I then
honestly stated that the new operation seemed to
be beyond his managerial ken. I made no recommend-
ations. That was one time when my blunt honesty
came hard to me. Mr. Packer was dismissed from
their employ, or allowed to resign, as the case
may be.

All in all, I enjoyed this project immensely and came away with the gratifying feeling of
a job well done. The place is beautiful and func-
tioning well. I have a tinge of pride whenever
I pass it.

XV. Government Work

XV. Government Work

The United States Government, as well as State
and City government, is considered by many consultants to be the mother lode for work and income. As I said before, I now shun work from that
quarter unless it is on an hourly or daily basis.
This, after hard and bitter experience.

All ongoing projects with the government require
contracts with endless stipulations in fine print.
Also, all require that you place yourself in a bidding situation against at least two other consultants or consulting firms. The answering of a bid
invitation in the form of a proposal is so complicated that it is sometimes necessary for the
government agency in question to accompany the
invitation with a thirty-page manual of instruc-
tions. You are not, of course, paid for the time
this takes.

I can readily understand how government can
make an intelligent decision regarding, for example, the purchase of aircraft, a service to
operate a canal, or paper clips. These are tangible things that can be judged primarily on the
basis of price and quality. But your work as a
consultant is so personalized that the agency
cannot make an *a priori* intelligent decision in
the form of a purchase order not much different
from the purchase order for paper clips. They
ask things like how many typewriter ribbons you
intend to use, exactly how much time you intend
to spend on the project, exactly how many telephone calls you intend to make, etc. Now, of
course, the only way to deal with nonsensical
questions is either with nonsensical answers or
by ignoring them altogether. Many consulting firms
have become masters at the game of nonsense. They
have acquired the art of writing gobbledygook
proposals which some government officials enjoy
receiving. A feasibility study on a feasibility
study is one of the favorites. But except for
the bottom line, i.e. your price *versus* your com-
petitor's, there is no way that the government
can come up with a choice for consultant. Using
price alone in our profession merely compares
apples with bananas.

So how does the government do it? This is
worth pursuing because here we have this one big
client that always pays its bills. In spite of

what we read about reform concerning the fairness
in awarding government contracts, when it comes
to contracting with consultants on fairly large
projects, you can pretty well take it for grant-
ed that over eighty percent of the contracts a-
warded are "wired". This means that the decision
has been made to do business with a particular
consulting firm long before the invitations to
bid are sent out. Of course, I could never prove
this in a court of law or at any official hearing. But I am satisfied that this is so, based
upon my own experience and the countless off-the-
record conversations I have had with government
employees. Satisfied enough, at least, to warn
you about it here.

You see, executives in government, in one
aspect at least, are not much different from executives in the private sector, when it comes to
doing business. They all have their own prefer-
ences regarding whom they want to do business
with. I certainly did, when I was an executive.
You probably do, too. Like average businessmen,
their choice is based either on reputation or on
first-hand knowledge having dealt successfully
with these same people before. But their agency
has a mandatory requirement that any job over a
certain budgetary amount (any big job) requires
an open bidding situation with at least three
contestants participating. This is why, at the
present time, I will only accept work below that

budgetary amount. I am hired, I work, and I am
paid.

Naturally, you are never told when a project
has been previously "wired" to someone else. The
agency official needs your proposal along with
that from at least one other schnook in order to
award the contract to the "wiree", and still play
by the book. It is a matter of form for him. This
sounds, and is, extremely unfair. But let's turn
the situation around. Suppose you had worked successfully for that agency before. Wouldn't you be
angry if you didn't automatically get the next
job? Or, suppose you had come to that agency with
an original brilliant proposal. How would you like
to have your proposal accepted contingent on the
fact that the agency would first have to circu-
late your idea to determine that it couldn't get
anyone else to carry it out at a cheaper price?
The whole system is rotten, either way you look
at it.

Example. I was once solicited by a very large
and prestigious federal agency to submit a proposal for doing an extensive survey. The young
lady who called told me that she was their new
evaluation officer. It seems that the agency had
not evaluated the efficacy of its own work since
its inception eight years before. (This should be
somewhat disconcerting to you, at the very least,
if you pay your taxes at all.) The first meeting

took place in my office. She asked for a detailed
budget forecasting all of my expenses and my exact
profit on the project. This "officer" told me that
the survey was to be in the form of an elaborate
questionnaire, that the information required was
to come from the realm of higher learning, and
that once the contract was awarded in early June,
the winning firm would have three months to gath-
er the information, collate it, evaluate it, and
write and publish the final report. I immediately
told her that a questionnaire would be fruitless
because (a) the halls of academe were virtually
empty during the summer months (for this one needs
the wisdom of a consultant?) and (b) no one of
any importance would give the enormous amount of
time gratis to fill out such a questionnaire
(more heavy advice here). This questionnaire
would have undoubtedly run ten pages to give us
the statistical information we required for mean-
ingful evaluation. This federal worthy allowed
as how this was all too true. I suggested that
there were other, more effective methods of getting the information. She asked that I detail
my methodology in my proposal. "You want me to
do all of this for nothing?" I asked incredulous-
ly. "Certainly," she said "the other nominees are
doing it." Well, I thought, maybe I was out of
step with the world as far as government work
was concerned. Let's give it a go and see what
happens. After the official assured me that she
was in complete agreement with me regarding the

worthlessness of a questionnaire and that any
firm that consented to do it that way would of
necessity have to fictionalize a final report
because of lack of information, I agreed to submit a detailed proposal and budget. I also made
her aware of the enormous pressures imposed upon
me by her limited time-frame to accomplish the
work. She said that it couldn't be helped because that final report was needed in order to
be incorporated into another report which had a
steadfast deadline.

Two months past the award date she had given
me, I heard nothing. I called her. She told me
that "the committee" had decided in favor of another firm, but, and these were her very words,
"thank you so much, Mr. Bermont, for helping us.
You know we *did* need several bids and it was so
difficult to find anyone who was qualified to do
this very specialized kind of work." Well, we
have a Freedom of Information Act now, so I was
able to find out who got the job and under what
conditions. It was awarded to a firm which proposed using a questionnaire. Also, that firm
was given two months longer to accomplish the
work than was I. Enough!

On the other side of the coin, I was called
one day by a government executive who asked if I
would be willing to go to Denver on a given date,
give a four-hour lecture at a seminar of 175

government people, and take on a one-hour ques-
tion-and-answer period. He agreed to my daily
fee plus expenses. I went. I worked. I was paid.

The President is now questioning what he
deems to be the useless hiring of consultants
by government agencies, not to mention the tremendous waste of taxpayer money. Hear, hear!
Government officials were supposed to be hired
or appointed for their expertise in their res-
pective fields in the first place. Whether the
President will be successful in the area is du-
bious. If not, and you like shenanigans, try to
hit the mother lode for a piece of the action and
spin your wheels. I still think you would have
a better chance with much less hassle at the two-
dollar window of your local race track.

XVI. Full Circle

XVI. Full Circle

Soon after the president of my former firm dismissed me (what seems like eons ago), he moved
up to an executive position in the owning conglo-
merate. A few years and a few presidents later
in the history of my former company, I received
a telephone call from the executive director of
our trade association. He had been requested to
find a replacement for that position, and asked
me if I wanted to be president. This director was
familiar with my work because the association itself had become one of my clients. My answer was
"They couldn't hire me for $50,000 a year. My
life is too beautiful." He said that $50,000 a
year was exactly what they were offering along
with benefits to start and that, although he
appreciated my attitude, he regretted my decision.
This episode is the kind of stuff that wish ful-
fillment dreams and waking fantasies are made of.
I extracted every ounce of delight from it. But

that wasn't all.

   A short time after that, my former superior
(president) called and invited me to lunch. We
hadn't talked since the time he fired me. Curios-
ity overcame hostility for the moment, and I accepted the invitation. He was not surprised, after ordering drinks and food (in a lovely restau-
rant, by the way), that his opening attempts at
small talk were falling on deaf ears. So he got
to the point. It seems that he had fallen out
of grace with the corporation, and he was now
shoved off into a corner (literally) with one
secretary, in charge of the smallest, most insig-
nificant part of the entire business. His contract
was terminating in a few months, and he had been
informed that it would not be renewed. In other
words, he himself had been fired. Recall that I
had bemoaned the fact that I had spent ten years
with the company before being sacked. This man
had given thirty-five years of his life to it.
Still and all, I could not find within myself
any compassion for him. Instead, I kept seeing
and hearing his fateful last meeting with his
superiors in my mind's eye and ear. Undoubtedly,
he was coldly told something like "You are going
nowhere with the company and the company is going
nowhere with you."

   He said that, because he was a shy, retiring
sort of person, and because I had become somewhat

well-connected in the industry during the past
few years, he would like to enlist my professional
services to help him find a job. I graciously
told him that I would see what I could do, but
that I would accept no fee, because I was a consultant, not a flesh-peddler. All the while, I
mused on his lack of self-awareness. A shy, retiring person doesn't abruptly dismiss an employee
after ten years of devoted service and then threat-
en to withhold his severance pay if the employee
doesn't lie to his staff by telling them that he
quit. Nor does a shy, retiring person take this
same former employee to lunch and calmly ask for
his help. To the contrary, this man had unmiti-
gated gall, and didn't even realize it.

In a few weeks, I heard of an opening and
called him. From an objective point of view, he
seemed to be right for the job, and I had never
questioned his competence. He applied, but didn't
get the position. Some time later, one of my clients
telephoned to ask my advice. It seems that my former boss had applied for a relatively unimportant
middle-management position in my client's firm
with the full knowledge that the salary was approximately half of what he was currently earning
in his job which was soon terminating. My client
was concerned. "Will he cut the mustard?" he asked, since I had worked so closely with the appli-
cant for so many years and knew him so well. I
honestly told my client that the risk wasn't all

that great. The subject in question was desperate, over fifty years of age, and experienced; he had to make it. He was duly hired. He has since moved to two different positions with two different companies.

Had I started to write a novel, instead of this book, I doubt that I could have plotted it better. They say that truth is stranger than fiction. I don't know. But I'm sure that in this eleven-year segment of my life, the truth has been more satisfying than fiction.

Partial List of Clients

Acropolis Books, Ltd.

A.F.of L.- C.I.O.

Air Force Association

American Association of Retired Persons

American Association of University Women

American Booksellers Association

American Federation of Teachers

American Film Institute

American Forest Institute

Ballantine Books

BFS Psychological Associates

B'nai B'rith

R.R. Bowker Company

The Brookings Institution

Catholic University

Chamber of Commerce of the United States

Data Solutions

Electronic Industries Association

Evelyn Wood Reading Dynamics

PARTIAL LIST OF CLIENTS

The Evening Star
Federation of American Societies for Experimental Biology
Garfinckels
Goodway
Grosset & Dunlap
Harper & Row
Human Events
Industrial Heating Equipment Association
International Reading Association
Journal of the Armed Forces
McGrath Publishing Company
McGraw-Hill
Metromedia
National Academy of Sciences
National Education Association
National Portrait Gallery
National Recreation & Park Association
National Retired Teacher's Association
National Wildlife Federation
Nation's Business
Optimum Book Marketing Company
Pitman Publishing Company
Performance Dynamics
Random House
The New Republic
Retired Officers Association
The Smithsonian Institution
Stein & Day
United States Department of the Interior
The Viking Press

WETA-TV

James T. White & Company